ANOTHER HEART TO ANOTHER

ISBN   978-0-9897657-1-8

PRINTED IN THE UNITED STATES OF AMERICA

ANOTHER HEART TO ANOTHER

Annette Whitaker-Moss

Rose Bud Imaginations

Rose Bud
Imaginations
The promise of new beginnings

www.annettewhitaker.com

Contents

WORDS OF WISDOM

Commit to the LORD whatever you do, and your plans will succeed.

Proverbs 16:3

In his heart a man plans his course, but the LORD determines his steps.

Proverbs 16:9

ACKNOWLEDGEMENTS

To My God

Father, I thank you for the precious gift of writing. May the words written by my hands inspire and motivate others, and always be pleasing in your sight.

To My Family

Your support and encouragement have been a big inspiration in my life. Thanks for always believing in me.

To My Friends and Spiritual Encouragers

I am so thankful that God put all of you in my life for a purpose. The unique bond that I share with each of you goes beyond measure of the appreciation, the friendship, and the love that we share.

SPECIAL THANKS TO MY CONTRIBUTORS

Editor – FirstEditing.com

Book Cover Designer – Rose Bud Imaginations

Artwork - www.clipartbest.com/calligraphy-borders

HONORS

My best friend…she has such a sweet and godly spirit that I respect and admire. God has blessed her with the gift of writing. Now, others can share in the richness of her blessings.

~Andrea Lightfoot

Another Heart to Another goes even deeper at peeling back layers to get to your most intimate feelings. It's reflective, it's personal, and I recommend it to anyone who has a heart.

~Debbie Ray

I'm blessed that I met Annette Whitaker-Moss during college and that we've become best friends. She's a sister in Christ, a beautiful, petite woman with a big heart. I'm so proud of her stepping out in faith and using her God-given talent in blessing others. After all, we're blessed to be a blessing (Genesis 12:2).

~Elaine Prejean
Unmasking Metastatic Breast Cancer

Annette, you are a fascinating, authentic poet. I feel you when I read your thought-provoking body of work. I am delighted because I get to call you my sister-friend too. I wish you well, and all of God's grace and mercy be on you. So proud of you.

~Paulette Bradford Wall-Harding

She is certainly gifted, and it is a privilege to have someone of her integrity and intellect, not to mention such a rich soul, to have as a colleague.

~Russel Hick

Keep Dreaming

Everyone will not always support your dreams.
Keep dreaming;
Amazed, you and all will see
When God plus you
Is all you need!

Annette Whitaker-Moss
06/13/13

A TRIBUTE TO MY DEAREST FRIEND

Paulette Bradford Wall-Harding
(8/11/1960 – 4/24/2017)

Today,
I smiled as I listened to the life you shared with so many others.
No doubt, my dearest friend, one-of-a-kind you have always been.
There was a special place in your heart for family, love ones, and friends
And this love for us, you demonstrated over and over again.

Tomorrow,
I will reminisce the laughter we shared throughout the years.
The good times and the bad times, the jokes and the tears
The plans, the dreams, expectations and the fears.
And the faith we shared that brought us through
These things, my dearest friend, I did with you.
You warmed my heart in all your glory
My wonderful, beautiful, loving, fun, and kindhearted friend,
I will always cherish what we shared deeply within.

Yesterday,
The angles watched over you,
Then, God made you an angel to watch over us too
The love we shared will always be,
In this life and throughout eternity.
Rejoice in heaven "Ms. Lady P"
On my mind and heart, you will always be.

Annette Whitaker-Moss
04/30/17

11

Rosebud

A tender rose is what I am
Redoubtable in every way.
My petals are colorfully expressed,
Sweetly scented, and uniquely tucked away.

In the center of my existence
As I genuinely unfold
I am the promise of new beginnings
Those that are told and untold.
Destroying me could never be
For I am represented by love
And, I blossom seasonally.

Annette Whitaker-Moss
02/21/14

"Your attitude and how you handle the things you go through in life is more important than the experience itself".

~ Quote by Annette Whitaker-Moss ~

Let Them Understand

Let not our children's hearts be harden
Or, their ears be deafened to the cause
Let them clearly understand
This temporary place we call home,
Is not the promise land.

Created to be conquers
To fulfill our Father's plan.
Let them not continue with their thinking,
That, they are in control of the master's plan.
Time will come and time will go
This was decided long ago.

Let not our children's hearts be harden
Or, their ears be deafened to the cause
Let them clearly understand
This temporary place we call home,
Is not the promise land.

Annette Whitaker-Moss
05/03/2017

14

A Sad Song "WHEN"

When the night planned for fun becomes loud voices and silent
screams,
The feelings for love are nowhere in between.
Emotions are trapped inside with nowhere to hide
And thoughts are wondering, this confusion, where will it lead?

When the small and meaningful things begin to disappear
Like sweet early morning kisses planted in your ear
And those on your cheek, while lying in bed, yet still asleep
Moments before the eyes have closed, innocent lips whisper,
"Goodnight," then reaches over and touches the other,
Hope is diminishing one step further.

When you are together and yet, you feel alone
Because communication and understanding are gone
You begin to face that all-too-familiar storm
Slowly progressing back to the past where sadness was the
norm.
It's where you swore you would never visit again
But, there you are, wondering, how did I not see all the signs in
front of me?
It's a very sad song when the love is gone!

Annette Whitaker-Moss
07/08/13

15

Apology

Analytical, I may be
But, also soft, loving, forgiving, and kind.
Strange sometimes, I know the world sees me
But, Thank God
That's not my destiny.

A tendency to carefully evaluate
As I try hard not to judge
Leaves my heart wide open
To lies and deceptions
That activate emotions, then words go unspoken.

Errors and flaws, we as people all share;
The difference is that some of us really do care.
When the worries of the world are pulling you down,
To you, I'd like to provide a smile, not a frown.

And if, for any reason
This, I did not accomplish,
I compassionately acknowledge
You are not an assumption.

So, understand as I state my plea;
Forgiveness must be of great sincerity.
I humbly offer to you, on this day
My deepest and loving apology.

Annette Whitaker-Moss
08/11/09

Be Strong

The eyes of the world may not always see
the beauty that lies inside of a wonderful, created mind as thee
But, do not fret!
The best is not seen yet.

Be strong in the Lord, my friend,
For the battle is not yours to win.
Sit back and relax
Till that time comes again
When the eye of all eyes
reveals his extraordinary plans.
Your life will certainly blossom and expand.

So, be strong
And know who you are!
Have faith,
And your dreams will go far.

The eyes of the world may not always see
the beauty that lies inside of a wonderful, created mind as thee
But, do not fret!
Instead, rejoice,
For the best is not seen yet.

Annette Whitaker-Moss
09/20/11

Beautiful, I Like To Be

Beautiful, I like to be
Inside and out for the world to see
With a glowing heart, a mindful soul,
A healthy body as I grow old.

Inspiring thoughts, I like to spread
Motivating, encouraging others to move ahead.
Pain killers, I like to release
using laughter to produce a sense of well-being thereafter.

Beautiful, I like to be
Inside and out for the world to see;
Great potential surrounding me
generously, with compassion, attention, and sympathy

Where love boldly stands next to me
Professing, providing, and protecting,
Understanding, I am a keeper
with standards and requirements, the world is seeking.

If the world could see inside of me,
Beautiful, I like to be.
Maybe a smile from one, two, or three
confirming this meekness and credibility,

Exquisite, I like to be
Where the Lord has searched and he knows me,
No signs of any liabilities
But, an imitation, fearfully and wonderfully made
This is what I like the world to see
If, it could see inside of me.

Annette Whitaker-Moss
03/17/09

18

Being in Love

When I can comment
And you don't frown,
Life for us will turn around.
When I can laugh and be myself,
There will be no room for anyone else.
If I can create a smile in you with just a thought,
Life with you will be as it ought.
When I can feel that we are one,
Accomplished love is what we've done.
Then, together, and being in love shall be fun!
'Cause understanding and accepting one another is
The beginning of being in love!

Annette Whitaker-Moss
02/16/14

Because

(Dedicated to Donald Moss)

Because I was so special to you
Even before, I knew
Because you saw potential happiness
and believe it to be true.

Because you brighten my life
with your beautiful smiles
And your gorgeous eyes set solely on me
Like no other before
I can clearly see
Us together throughout earth's eternity.

Because you gave, so freely, every part of you
This warmth inside, it grew and grew
And suddenly, I knew
My prayers had been answered
You are my dream come true!

Because on Easter, April 4, 2010
You initiated a lifetime;
A new beginning, middle, and end,
A friendship,
A courtship,
A soon-to-be partnership,
Faithfully knowing that we shall transcend
Because, we, together, are a perfect blend.

Because we tend to love unconditionally
as we help and comfort one another
In times of prosperity and adversity
Our loyalty, honesty, and trust
will lead us to our destiny.

It's how you tell the story of our beginning;
With strong faith and hope of us never ending.
For all of these many, precious reasons
You are my "because"
that will last through every season.

Annette Whitaker-Moss
08/06/10

Bold, Dark, Beautiful Dancer

Boldly, he observes
And silently, he smiles.
Selecting each girl, one by one
Next in line, to learn and have some fun.
Alternative walk, chi, chi, chi,
Again, he stares and catches my eye.

Who is this bold, dark, beautiful dancer?
With a smooth and carefree soul,
Enthusiastic and motivated
To accelerate and demonstrate
His own personal moves and goals?

Dark, tall, Dutch chocolate with hot fudge
Bald head, smooth beard
Confident and masculine
With his silver 1-carat diamond stud.

Ooh! What's next?
Basic steps
Behind the back
Let's rehearse
She turns, he turns
Stationary, reverse
Quickly, I peep, as I am shy.
Again, he stares and catches my eye
Bold, dark, beautiful dancer
Could you, someday, be my guy?

Annette Whitaker-Moss
08/12/09

Born To....

Born with a heart and the ability to feel
sadness, pain, and laughter, but able to be healed.
Born to be loved and to love others,
To give and forgive with the ability to understand,
to correct and guide further.

Born to choose the difference between right and wrong
To live together or apart
To smile or frown
To open or close our minds of our surroundings,
To lend a helping hand or turn away,
To dream, to hope, and to believe
Birth itself, was created to achieve.

Annette Whitaker-Moss
03/28/09

Complicated

How does one explain such a caring soul?
Who knows and understands that love is patient and kind,
Not rude, self-seeking or easily angered,
Does not delight in evil but rejoices in truth,
Protects, trusts, hopes, and perseveres
For these wonderful things of God I thought I saw in you.

And yet, a complicated man you can sometimes be,
Listens, but does not hear or accept humor;
Understands and exhibits concern, but counts it all as danger.
Simple and truthful words spoken, yet you foresee them as threatening.
Opinionated, even though you think you're not.
Judging, criticizing, and condemning others,
But it is taught, we must first remove the speck from our own eyes before we will clearly see the speck in another's.

These words, in your mind, may confirm that I am not the one for you.
For I am simple, straightforward, loving, and fun, too.
This is how I was made, there's no other me.
God made me this way for a purpose, you see,
And to most, to know me, is to love me.
For this, God knows, I truly thank thee!

Annette Whitaker-Moss
03/08/10

Counting Down

One year has passed
And though I saved the best for last
I fear my time is running out fast.
There is no unity,
There is no intimacy,
There is no joy,
Only distance setting in from afar.

How long will it be?
My eyes cannot foresee.
My senses are strong and surrounding me,
Sending unpleasant vibes, challenging me,
Reminding me to keep the faith
And remain faithful,
For the best is yet to come.

Still, I argue.
My heart is wounded.
A year later and six months counting,
Nothing, not even a touch.
Expressing nothing to disclose.
Three months and I am no longer the rose.
Pampered and surrounded with gratification;
What more before it comes to a close?

Annette Whitaker-Moss
12/01/13

Dancing With the One

Are you the one?
I would spend the remaining of my life
Dancing, smiling, and romancing
With your silver beard and mustache,
Your bald head and elegant class.

Smooth, light-chocolate, butter pecan
Eyes that sparkle with so much charm
As I twist and turn into the side basic.
She turns, he turns, and then we're facing
Eye to eye;
Beautiful lady,
Awesome guy!

Alternative walk has now begun.
My arm around your waist, as we turn,
Rotating back,
Preparing to sway
As we dance this night away,
Anticipating another day!

Annette Whitaker-Moss
07/06/09

My Daughter

God made no mistakes when he blessed us with you.
I'm thankful, daughter,
He gave us one another
So we could bond and mend our hearts together.

The road was not always easy;
It was not always fun.
But being a mother captures the essence of each and everyone
No matter the outcome,
No matter the struggle.
There is always love between you and me, daughter and
mother.

Putting you in God's hands was the only way to let go
So you would get on the right path in order for you to grow.
It was the only thing I knew
And the only thing to do.

Wanting only the best for you at the highest degree,
I, your mother, leading and guiding before your time to flee,
I was praying and asking God, please watch over thee
As you discover your own prayers, challenges, mistakes, and
victories,
I hope you fall into the plans God has had for centuries.

Jeremiah 29:11 – *For I know the plans I have for you,
declares the LORD, "plans to prosper you and not to harm
you, plans to give you hope and a future".*
------------------L O V E,   M O M------------------

Annette Whitaker-Moss
12/04/12

27

Do Nothing but Your Best

As you begin this wonderful quest,
Remember to always do your best.
Nothing in life is to be feared
For God did not give us the spirit of fear
He gave us knowledge,
A way to obtain understanding.
He gave us a heart,
A way to fulfill his eternal purpose.
He gave each of us positive attributes,
Talents, so we all may contribute
With virtue, ambition, and righteousness.

Traveling not alone
Through the journey of despair or success
We are expected to do nothing but our best;
God will take care of the rest
For we are his creation
And he planned the perfect process.
Remember to always do your best
And let God take care of the rest.

Annette Whitaker-Moss
04/17/12

Don't Sell Me Out

Daddy, don't sell me out 'cause of what your eyes may see.
Because you love me, look beyond what it appears to be.
Remember, you are the one who raised me;
Show rejoice for the son you've gotten.
Have confidence in things you taught
Understanding your prayers for me are not forgotten.

Your expectations I will surely meet;
The journey I'm on does not lead to defeat.
Allow me to learn, grow, and make mistakes
At my pace
Not yours
And with God's good grace.

Don't sell me out
Because of your doubt.
Walk by faith;
Believe, and everything will surely work out.

Don't sell me out 'cause of what your eyes may see.
Because you love me,
Look beyond what it appears to be.

Annette Whitaker-Moss
01/10/12

Emotional Roller Coaster

Today, I will miss you.
Tomorrow, I probably won't speak to you.
Yesterday, I longed for you, my heart ached.

Joy, sometimes finds me.
Love, always seems to wonder.
Hate, I can't seem to do.
Yet, I'm lost without you.

When will I hear from you?
How will I truly know you?
Where will my love go with you?
My spirit mourns.

What is it that makes me ignore all the signs?
Lack of dedication,
Unfaithfulness,
Total despair.

How can it be that I am so blind?
It seems you just don't care.
I really don't know;
But, it's like an emotional roller coaster
Up and down we go.

Annette Whitaker-Moss
10/16/06

Everything Hurts

The lack of words,
Too many words,
The pretending,
The loneliness,
Togetherness,
The sight of you,
Missing you.

Is it love?
Or a mistake?
Do I care?
It's isn't hate.
But, how do I escape?
'Cause everything I feel
Just really seems to hurt.

Annette Whitaker-Moss
08/13/13

Exterior/Interior

Today, Lord,
The level of frustration is high.
The human exterior wants to act, curse, scream, hurt someone or just be mean.
Somehow, the interior side is calm, forgiving, patient, and part of this wonderful work in progress.
Learning to love, learning to be patient, learning to be kind and not envious,
Not boasting, nor swollen with pride.

Today, Lord,
I just needed to be reminded of the things you've hidden in my heart.
To be still and wait on you, because you will always do your part.
To be thankful for your grace and mercy.
Though, weeping may endure for a night
But, joy comes in the morning
So there's no need to ponder with fright.

Today, Lord,
I will concentrate on you, so the nuisances will be few.
The human exterior will be patient, doing nothing, but yearning for your guidance.
The reactions shall tell your story to magnify your name.
The interior side will be smiling, while bonding together as one
Realizing now, that they are one and the same.

Annette Whitaker-Moss
03/07/12

Farewell, My Friend

(Dedicated to Berlene Williams)

We were blessed
To know one another as friends.
We shared your child together,
You, as mother,
Me, as godmother,
To care and love always, until the end.

The heart expressed what no other can see.
It's intimate and personal for eternity
For God knows best
From all the rest
Indeed, you were a friend to me
And I to you.
You trusted me with your child, you see
And made me her mother too.

Now, I have not one, but three;
A daughter, granddaughter, grandson
Granted to me from your legacy.
So rest in peace, my friend,
Let not your soul be troubled.
Every call made now and then
Told how much you really loved us.

Annette Whitaker-Moss
01/07/10

Game

The Player....
Says the sweetest things,
Only words without a meaning,
Pretend it's all good,
Simply misunderstood,
Cares less who gets hurt,
It's only a flirt,
Prerogative on the mind,
Promiscuous, all the time.

The Inexperienced....
Glows over the smallest things.
Words of beauty,
Compassion, has such meaning
Spoken as no other would
Never think of getting hurt
Enjoying every word, every flirt,
Sincerity on the mind,
Faithful, all the time.

The Experienced....
Hears and recognizes game,
Plays along just the same.
Been down that road once or twice,
Most obvious now is the device.
Walk away from the game
Do not play;
Worth is well known.
Deserves better – desires better.
Demands better – seeks better.
Finds better!

Game over!

Annette Whitaker-Moss
06/08/09

34

Harmony

I can win your trust
I can win your respect
But, I'm aiming for your heart
'Cause, it's love I expect.

You, learning my love language
And I will learn yours,
A heartfelt commitment is what I desire
And what I deserve!

I can win your trust,
I can win your respect,
But, I'm aiming for your heart
'Cause, it's love I expect.

Annette Whitaker-Moss
05/03/07

I Am Not

I am <u>not</u> second best!
God created me to uplift, inspire, and to shine
Like silver and gold.
Not to hide behind the rest, wasting my years
As I grow old.

I am bold;
I expect the best!
I am strong;
I accept nothing less.
God's word will not guide me wrong.
I believe and receive;
I am <u>not</u> second best!

I am beautiful
And wonderfully made
To glow as I sparkle
For the world to see.
This man, when he comes for me
I will know, God made him, just for me.

He will smile
And proudly walk beside me.
He will hold my hand, protecting, providing,
And professing the blessing that I am.
The girl he chose to uphold, to marry, to love.
I believe and receive
He put me above the rest
'Cause I am <u>not</u> second best!

Annette Whitaker-Moss
09/16/11

I Have Nowhere Else To Go

Relentless tears
For a broken heart,
A nemesis to my soul.
A cry for relief,
A peaceful night's sleep;
I have nowhere else to go.

Pleading release
The appearance of hidden joys
Causing body aches and loneliness,
Unattainable emotions;
I have nowhere else to go.

Once, I was loquacious
Now filled with paranoia.
Will my life go back to normal?
Deep in thought I ponder
I have nowhere else to go.
I beseech you, Lord,
The world's highest counselor!
I have nowhere else to go.

Annette Whitaker-Moss
01/16/14

I Remember Thinking

I remember thinking, one day,
Lord, I've gone astray.
I walk different,
I talk different,
I act different.
What is it that caused me to change?
My heart knows this behavior is insane.

Is it the company I keep?
And that I've fallen behind with your practice
and studies?
Trying to keep up with society as I compete.
I remember thinking, oh, my God!
I've become a little lost sheep!

But, all is not lost.
This, I remember thinking,
My Father paid the cost
so, there's no need to continue this sinking.

Yes, I've gone astray,
But I came back on this very day.
I was taught the right way.
The word is hidden in my heart
and I know, faith and I shall never part.

And even though
I've stooped so low
I remember thinking
My Father still loves me so.

I fell to my knees
And spoke from my heart,
I asked for forgiveness
Then, thanked him for deliverance!

Annette Whitaker-Moss
01/11/12

It's Easy to See Me

It's easy to see me
For I possess the qualities of loyalty.
My friends and loved ones are like diamonds,
Precious and priceless,
Worthy of my praise, concern, and recognition.
With them, I share and care for all eternity.

My smile can lighten the mood.
My ears will listen and display trustworthiness.
My mouth will speak with caution.
But my tongue has no limits as my heart strives
to motivate happiness, joy, and understanding
the essence of love and longevity.

Forgiveness is a necessity.
I cling not long to grudges.
Knowing my own temperament,
I appreciate my strengths and weaknesses.
With patience, I use these attributes to encourage
myself and others.
To walk by faith and not by sight,
for the journey of life could turn out be a very
long hike.

My priorities are in order:
God, family, friends,
and the love I share individually with each and
every one of them.
These are the qualities that I possess.
It's easy to see me, I must confess.
But, if you look for me and cannot find me
Please, by all means, feel free to protest.
I'd rather know now than be put to the test.

Annette Whitaker-Moss
05/30/14

Just Because

Just because....
You really, really, like him
That isn't enough to invite him into your heart.
Into your mind, your soul, or into your world.

Will he profess his love?
Will he protect your love?
Will he provide and respect your love?
Or just make your head twirl?

Just because....
He whispers the sweetest words.
Even says, "I'm crazy about you, girl."
That isn't enough to decide if he's unattached,
If he's trustworthy, willing to commit,
Or, if he understands your worth.

Just because....
Isn't enough
To turn your life upside down
Over someone who's a little kind
And always on your mind.

Will he put into motion the things he says?
If not, just because is a lot,
But not enough!

Annette Whitaker-Moss
06/29/09

Life Began To Change

So many days I thought of giving up.
Children are raised as they should,
But, chose the way of the world,
Not understanding how great they are
Fearfully and wonderfully made
To be conquerors of this universe
As our Father had planned and rehearsed.

Then, I remembered
I was once that child who knew it all;
How life should be.
I was blind and could not see
This extraordinary life
Our Father created for me.

And through it all
Mistakes were made
That led me far from my destiny.
Still, our Father did not given up on me
Though he chastised me along the way
His love never strayed.

Finally, the day came;
I realized all the hurt, pain, and shame
And asked, Lord, could you ever forgive
And trust me once again?
He smiled, and my life began to change.

Annette Whitaker-Moss
04/08/11

43

Light

Let there be light, said the Lord,
Igniting brightness over the whole universe,
Glorifying his wonder,
Highly recognizing his phenomenal creation,
Thunder and lightning, hear him roar!

Enlightening to all mankind
Light, as it represents God's love
Manifests all things, life and death,
Assigned to goodness, as darkness is to evil,
Light is energy for all life's sequels.

Annette Whitaker-Moss
10/2/2015

Listen

Pouring out the misery that lies heavily on my heart
Consistently, I say to you, listen before I depart.
If you truly love me,
The pain I am experiencing will not be ignored.
What man wants to relinquish the creation of flame, fire, and passion
in the woman he says he loves?

Weary, I've become, waiting for a different response,
Tempted every day to feel alive and be desired again.
Anxious, I am, for a new and exciting life to begin.
Intentionally, I ask you,
Be that person igniting the spark that lies dormant within.
But, as usual, I get the same reaction:
No care, no concern, no passion!

Listen, life is just too short.
Listen, before you leave me no choice.
Listen, hear, and understand me
Before the day comes when I shall depart.

Annette Whitaker-Moss
07/01/15

Little Black Sheep

Our little black sheep,
We love you so dearly
You must wake up
So you can see clearly.
Open your eyes
So you will see;
Search deep inside, within your heart
and know, love surrounds you and will never part.

But, there's only so far love can go.
There comes a time when only you can help yourself,
When God, your mind, and soul are in tune with no one else.
Don't be blind, for there's very little time
to renew your mind.
Intelligence is granted to all mankind.

You have the strength to turn your life around.
Fear and depression have no ground.
We will stand together in faith
with our prayer warriors,
And praise God for your victory and his honors.

You have eyes of beauty,
A mind full of potential.
You are so precious.
We want to keep you,
Our little black sheep.
Hear our plea.
We love you so dearly.
You must wake up
So, you can hear clearly.

Annette Whitaker-Moss
01/07/10

Loquacious People

Loquacious people
Sometimes are hard to deal with.
Some are pejorative,
Never realizing the goodness in others.
Never experiencing what others have to offer.
Never hearing with an open heart.

Some are opinionated,
Never seeing beyond their own beliefs,
Expecting some sort of change
In others, but not themselves.
Because what they see is fault in someone else,
Never substantial fault in themselves.

Some are selfish
And intolerant towards others,
Imposing their innermost feelings,
Not knowing that some are unforgiven.
Someday, maybe someday,
They will realize.

People are different for a reason.
People are given the right
To imagine, to explore,
To be unlike any other.
To live in their own way.
Then face the ultimate judgment day.

Annette Whitaker-Moss
03/02/14

Love and No Regrets

A love affair was secretly enhanced
The first time I heard your name,
When we laughed, played, sang, and danced
My heart knew it was the beginning of a new romance.

You overwhelmed me with joy,
Protected me from harm's way,
Made it known I was your girl
Inside a huge and crazy world.

Every day with you, life is complete.
Many nights I dream of you as I sleep.
When morning comes, I eagerly seek
Your honesty, courtesy, friendship, and respect,
Knowing I will love you even more with no regrets.

Annette Whitaker-Moss
05/29/11

Love Looked Good on Me

I remember when love <u>looked</u> good on me.
My face shone like the comforting moon of the night,
Impulses traveled from my head to my toes
And I felt the smile of assurance
As it covered me with love.

Though envy surrounded me,
Still, best wishes followed me
For longevity and admiration
A complete connection and sensation
Filled daily with bliss
and sealed with one single kiss.
I remember when love <u>looked</u> good on me.

Neglect was lost in the wind
Never finding a chance to sneak in.
Imperfections were invisible to the eyes
Smoothing all of my unwanted cries.
The sound of laughter is what I heard
While wined and dined
with cheese, crackers, and hors d'oeuvres.
Sirloin steak or lobster,
all the meals that I deserved.
I remember when love <u>looked</u> good on me.

Annette Whitaker-Moss
03/22/14

Misconception of Society

The media focuses heavily on robberies, drugs, and killings
While portraying black society as the villains.
How can we be so simple-minded?
Believing blacks are the primary criminals?
Why? It's a misconception of society
And now, our society is suffering drastically by the millions.
When will our society understand?
That yes, black lives matter.
When will our society demand a change?
Because all lives matter.
When will our society comprehend?
That God created all human beings.
It was He who created this world for you and for me.
When will our society recognize?
God's desire for a diverse society.
It was his choice for us not to be identical.
Therefore, we must all change so we don't become so cynical.
Why are we blinding the cries of the black society?
By focusing solely on the officers in blue
While their families matter, other families matter too.
Punish those who are wrong
All colors, whether black or blue
We must all stand in unity to win this fight.
"One nation, indivisible, with liberty and justice for all."
That is our Pledge of Allegiance.
That is our challenge, as the people, for we have been called!

Annette Whitaker-Moss
10/10/16

My Hands Are Blessed

You're provided the knowledge
You gave me the talent
You've given me faith
And hope that is valid.

Confirmation has begun
To go above and beyond
With your blessings.
I've already succeeded!
With your love
I've already won.

With that being said,
Father, I thank you,
For the works of my hands are blessed.
My heart craves your approval
To carry along this beloved quest.

'Cause you've given me what is needed
To recognize and glorify
The grace that supersedes
All my shortcomings
So that my hands are blessed
In your authority
And no other can protest.

Annette Whitaker-Moss
11/15/11

My Valentine

The sparkle of my life,
Symbolic of a rose,
Precious as precious can be,
Adorable and sweet; all can see
You mean the world to me.

Such an awesome pair;
Our love is unique, beyond compare
As our hearts together unite as one.
Every day of happiness I will seek to bring
To you, my sweetheart, my everything.

One of a kind, you are to me.
On my mind, you will always be
My special, my sweet, my loving, my darling,
Valentine!

Annette Whitaker-Moss
03/04/06

Our Love Would Have Lasted

You stole my heart with your gentleness,
Your smile, your kindness, and your desire to please.
But along the way, your soul turned cold
And my heart began to bleed.

In disbelief, my heart was frozen;
Would this storm find its end?
Your soul turned colder than ice,
So cold, I found no mending within.

Had I known you as a rubber band,
Able to bend and weather the storm,
Someone who could take the heat
Stand strong and be flexible,
Knowing the rainbow would soon be showing.

Had you been willing and forgiving,
Choosing wisely as you conquer all challenges.
Had we stood together and fought for each other
Your smile, your kindness, and your desire to please
Would have overwhelmed me
And brought me to my knees.

Our love would have lasted
I know, with faith of a mustard seed,
Our love would have succeeded.

Annette Whitaker-Moss
06/09/14

54

Perfect Christmas Gift

Couldn't imagine my first Christmas gift to you,
A personalized silver pen, key ring, and a business card case will do
But then, I thought maybe something tender, playful,
passionate, and challenging too.

All these things I see in me
A perfect combination of originality
Someone to match your humor
Your personality
Your caring nature
And your friendliness, too
And suddenly, it came to me.

What a perfect gift to give!
Words of expression,
Something to keep close to your heart
From me to you as we share together
This hope of growing closer each passing year and forever.

H A P P Y   H O L I D A Y S

Annette Whitaker-Moss
12/03/08

55

Possibilities

Gently, he grabs me around my waist,
Effortlessly, he spins me around,
Romantically, he dips me once, then twice
Lifting me softly as he gazes into my eyes,
and I smile.
Now I know anything is possible!

Annette Whitaker-Moss
10/16/16

Praying for Rain in 2011

Praying for rain, dear Lord.
A relief from all this heat.
The yards and fields have all dried up
Causing fires and many fears.
Still, we know there's hope, not defeat.

Meteorologists have no control.
They only track and report what they are told
But, you, dear Lord, with just a word
Command nature to obey and perform what is heard.

There's none other on whom we can depend
To save us from a dreadful end.
Forgive us, Lord, for all our sins.
Help us, Lord, to make amends.
Have mercy on us, Lord, so we may blend
All that you have given us to glorify its beauty once
again!

Annette Whitaker-Moss
09/20/11

Qualities of a Husband

Holding their wife's hands
And sharing their hearts,
They are the running boards, missing from the trucks
Lifting their wife high enough for them to step up

When the doors are opened
Rooms are filled with roses,
Beautiful colors, coordinated and exposed for everyone
who notices.

Attention is given to the lady in their life
For there are no other women
This special lady
Everyone knows
Is his wife.

Covered with protection
Flattered with affection
Dressed in love
With a husband who leads and guides in the right direction
And for this reason, his wife respects him.

Thank you, God, for this magnificent husband!

Annette Whitaker-Moss
06/13/13

Remembering the Voice

Patience didn't follow me in this morning.
My happy face was there, but not patience.
When I arrived, I sat in my chair
and my computer gave me quite a scare.

It was flashing off and on,
Sending error messages here and there,
Opening and closing tabs with every click
sending me signals to be aware.

I was huffing and puffing
Unaware of my surroundings,
Being very inconsiderate
'Cause patience didn't follow me in this morning.

Then, a voice said to me.
"I will call you every morning and remind you to bring your friend."
Baffled, but still I asked, "What friend?"
Softly and gently, the voice responded, "Patience."
And suddenly, I became me again!
Thank God for these types of voices…for some are called friends!

Annette Whitaker-Moss
09/12/14

Respect and Adore

I respect the man:

He opens doors
Helps me in and out of the car
Watches over me
Protects me from remarks and harm
Frequently, he cooks and cleans
Buys me things he wants me to have
He holds my hand
Takes me to the movies and out to eat
He stands tall and proud beside me
Professing that he loves and cares for me
He does what he can to provide for me
He attends church with me
And dresses in the same colors as me for the day.

I respect the husband when he does that and more:

He's always striving to have a relationship with God
So when difficult times approach, he knows how to talk
with God and delight in his promises.
He knows by pleasing God first, all else will follow.
He goes over and beyond as a provider for me.
When he studies every part of me,
He discovers my natural scent of intimacy;
My heart's reaction during arousal, plateau, and orgasm.
When he knows my love languages,
He comprehends my needs, my wants, my joys, and is
not afraid to make them a reality.

When he holds me tight, as needed
He warms my heart and brings me comfort.
He's not afraid to explore me and take me places I've
never been before; physically, mentally, and spiritually.

So, I respect the man, but I respect and adore the husband
who does more!

Annette Whitaker-Moss
10/11/16

My Son

I thank God, son,
You gave me no problems
Growing up, while you were young.
You amazed me with your charisma
And always made my heart feel warm.

A late bloomer, you were,
So it appeared, as your peers left you behind.
But overnight you became the young, mature
man, destiny was sure to find.

You launched into life with a mind of your own
Still respectful, while abiding my wishes.
You left very few things that caused me to frown.
Don't get me wrong, my son,
A few of those issues were opinionated, and very long.
It was a battle we knew only one of us could have won.

Victory is what the two of us seek.
You, a young man trying to reach his peak.
I, your mother, seeing what you had yet to see,
Wanting only the best for you at the highest degree,
Trying to lead and guide before your time to flee.
I was praying and asking God, please watch over thee.

Soon I realized it was time to let go.
Putting you in God's hands was the only way to do so.
As you discover your own prayers, challenges, mistakes, and victories.
I hope you fall into the plans God has had for c enturies.

Jeremiah 29:11 *- For I know the plans I have for you, declares the LORD, "plans to prosper you and not to harm you, plans to give you hope and a future ".*

------------------L O V E M O M------------------

Annette Whitaker-Moss
12/04/12

I Love the Sweet and Meaningful Things

Like the sweet early morning kisses planted on my
cheek while lying in bed, yet still asleep.
Or, just before my eyes have closed, innocent lips
whisper "good night" then reach over and touch
the other.

Anticipation of creative lovemaking
With exciting and intriguing orgasms
Sending the glow of delight throughout
every particle of my body.

The feel of your lips
Beginning at my temple,
Headed towards my cheeks,
Landing on my earlobes,
Moving towards my toes,
Exploring my reactions, waiting to explode!

The fragrance of love
And déjà vu signals
Putting a smile on my face,
Making me delusional with thoughts of
every move from the night before!

The aftermath,
The pillow talks,
The whispers,
The laughter.

I love the sweet and meaningful things!

Annette Whitaker-Moss
07/08/13

Still, Oh Lord

My heart speaks to you, oh Lord,
For I have not been as I should.
Still, I thank you that my life is not as it could.

For I am not hungry
I am not alone
I am not homeless
I am not ill
I am not forgetful of who you are.
My heart and soul yearns for you still.

Thank you for being who you are
And thank you for letting me know whose I am;
A child of yours
Whom you have wonderfully made.

My heart speaks to you, oh Lord,
For I have not been as I should.
Still, I thank you that my life is not as it could.

Annette Whitaker-Moss
11/13/11

Talent

Give a little of yourself
To help encourage someone else.
Talent isn't given because we are so deserving,
It's given to use for the good and care of others.
There's no need to be conserving.
Talent is to be shared with all our sisters and our brothers.
Remember, it's given to use for the good and care of others.

Annette Whitaker-Moss
07/10/11

Sweet Sixteen - The Coming of Age

(Dedicated to Empris Durden)

The coming of age
Commences a new page of responsibilities,
Privileges, and possibilities.

Sweet sixteen
Yes, you are!
Beautiful, courageous,
A shining star!

Approach the world with self-confidence
Because you have the trait of discipline
To make decisions of great consequence.

As you transition from childhood to adulthood
Overcome the test of strength
With endurance and assurance
That God is closer than arm's length.

Life is challenging
And exciting too.
It depends on whatever
You choose to do.

Just remember
It's fun being a teen
So, be sixteen
But act like a queen
And most of all stay focused
And accomplish all your dreams!

Annette Whitaker-Moss
06/13/11

The MFA Family

(Martin Fletcher & Associates)

Here at MFA
People recognize, motivate, and strive
To make a difference each and every day,
Setting examples for all to see,
Conveying the message of prosperity.

Be healthy, be wealthy, and be wise,
Revealing that state of mind that wins the ultimate prize.
Excellence is what we seek;
The need of self and others is what we meet.

Proudly called MFA
Where selfishness and pride we tuck away.
We work hard, and then we play,
Nourishing and refreshing ourselves
As we start a new day
To create a health care community
Where we can all rise
And thrive in unity.

Annette Whitaker-Moss
07/08/11

Undeniable

I am a woman;
Valuable
Desirable
And undeniable

When your focus isn't blinded with actions
towards my happiness,
Or your heart isn't grieving when I am displeased,
When our bodies speak a foreign language that's
not in unison
And you no longer desire my uniqueness,
When every woman is beautiful, kind, and sweet,
Deserving of your eyes, smile, and meekness,
Then, you are not for me.

I am a woman;
Valuable
Desirable
And undeniable.

Annette Whitaker-Moss
12/12/14

Unforgettable You

Unforgettable, wonderful you.
A chance online, who knew?
In this day and time such a relationship, it grew
From a simple hello and how are you
To the first date, a Maverick's game
Unforgettable, wonderful you.

Elegant restaurants you exposed me to.
Rick Stein, Mi Piaci, McGuire, and Oceannaire,
Message therapies and body treatments,
Cards, roses, lilies, flowers, and bouquets,
These are the things that you have shared,
Unforgettable, wonderful you.

Front-row seats to the amazing Maze and Tyler Perry.
A chance online, who knew?
One year, three months ago,
Pretty, sexy, and desirable would somehow meet
Unforgettable, wonderful you.

Annette Whitaker-Moss
06/25/08

Well-Established Man

The boldness and the confidence of a well-established man
Are appealing to the mind and heart of a woman.
He leaves no unfinished business behind;
No negative attitudes, anxiety, or fears.
He appears with compassion,
He is respectful and he is kind!

Annette Whitaker-Moss
07/08/13

71

Why Would You Not?

Why would you not put a smile on her face?
Not like a colleague, a companion, or a pal
But one who travels from her mind, her body, to her heart
and deeply touches her soul as well.
Let it reach and touch her innermost thoughts
And boldly speak, "I've got your every need."
"You are my one and only, my true love indeed."

Why would you not treasure her like a pearl?
Making her feel like a natural, beautiful woman.
Refining her into a magnificent diamond
as you lighten her burdens and relieve her stress.
While motivating and inspiring her to do her best,
Reaching and touching her innermost thoughts
While boldly speaking, "I've got your every need."
"You are my one and only, my true love indeed."

Why would you not embrace her spirituality?
As she walks not as a carnal Christian
But one who walks by faith and not by sight,
Desiring all good things: God's grace and favor,
protection, peace, health, joy, pleasure, and wealth,
As you reach and touch her innermost thoughts
While boldly speaking, "I've got your every need."
"You are my one and only, my true love indeed."

Why wouldn't you keep her wondering about the future?
So maybe, she can forget about her past,
Or bond with her in lovemaking that's oh so ever sweet,
Giving her a vision each night as she lays down to sleep,
Reminding her with a whisper that your love will forever keep,
Reaching and touching her innermost thoughts
While boldly speaking, "I've got your every need."
"You are my one and only, my true love indeed."

Why would you not put a smile on her face?
Causing her to glow from head to waist,
Melting from waist to toes, hoping everyone knows
She can never deny,
Your love fulfilled her every desire.
Because you reached out and touched her innermost thoughts
While boldly speaking, "I've got your every need."
"You are my one and only, my true love indeed."

Annette Whitaker-Moss
5/17/16

Yesterday, Today, Tomorrow

Yesterday, I saw you
And pretended all was well.
I smiled as you glanced my way,
Flirting and gloating with your new girl.

Today, I think I will grieve
The loss of my lover, my friend,
And deal with the sadness felt deeply within.

Tomorrow will be a new beginning for me.
I will look at you and see you very differently.
No more laughter and playful moments,
For these memories, I vow today,
I gently and safely tuck them away.

Yesterday, it happened, and I cried.
Today, I dried my tears and conquered my fears.
Tomorrow, I'll prepare my heart once again
So joy, laughter, and happiness may find its way in.

Annette Whitaker-Moss
04/08/10

You Pledged Your Life

I never asked to marry you.
You knelt down on one knee
And pledged your life to me,
Promising to love and cherish
For the whole world to see.

To believe in the splendid,
To rejoice in the genuineness
of the admiration from your heart,
Providing security for my well-being
My personality
My sensuality
And my imperfections
Not for one year, two years, or three
But for all eternity

You asked me
And I agreed
I became your wife to be
'Cause you pledged your life to me.

Annette Whitaker-Moss
02/01/14

Do You Still Love Me?

If, so...
Where is the intimacy that a woman hungers for;
desire, not neglect?
     Where is the fragrance of love?
     Sending déjà vu signals to my senses
     Putting a smile on my face
     Making me delusional with thoughts
     Of every move from the night before?

Where is the anticipation of creative lovemaking?
     With exciting and intriguing orgasms
     Sending the glow of delight throughout
     Every particle of my body?

Where is the gentle massage from your lips?
     Beginning at my temple
     Headed towards my cheeks
     Landing on my earlobes
     Moving towards my toes
     Exploring my reactions, waiting to explode?

What happened to the aftermath?
     The pillow talks?
     The whispers?
     The laughter?

Do you still love me? If so, I need...
     The intimacy
     The fragrance of love
     The anticipation of creative lovemaking
     The gentle massage from your lips
     And the aftermath.

These are the unspoken words
Speaking to my heart
Promising, we as one will never part
Do you still love me?

Annette Whitaker-Moss
06/30/13

Words

Words are powerful, as they provoke our <u>thinking.</u>
They direct our <u>emotions</u>; our natural instinctive state of mind.
Virtuous or corrupt, worldly or spiritual, loving or kind,
Prompting <u>actions</u> that lead to <u>habits</u>; improvement or destruction
While determining our <u>character,</u> and conveying our <u>destiny.</u>
Words are meanings deeply rooted in our minds.

For some, meanings are hidden, and others proven true.
Some become unsympathetic, while others, they understand
Words are vital, essential, significant, and momentous too,
Exposing our mind, body, and soul.
Meaningful beauty is hidden inside the words we use
And, the words we are told.

Annette Whitaker-Moss
11/9/2016

www.ingramcontent.com/pod-product-compliance
Lightning Source LLC
Chambersburg PA
CBHW041529090426
42738CB00035B/5